Tales from the
Arabian Nights

Simplified by John Turvey

Illustrated by Jeroo Roy

850 word vocabulary

Longman

Longman Group Limited
Longman House
Burnt Mill
Harlow
Essex
U.K.

First published 1963
New edition 1983

ISBN 0 582 52838 0

Printed in Singapore by
Ban Wah Press Pte Ltd

Contents

CHAPTER ONE

The Sultan and Sheherezade

Sultan Shahriar had a beautiful wife. She was his only wife, and he loved her more than anything in the world. Some people said that he loved her too much; and perhaps they were right, because she was not as good as she seemed. The Sultan's love was not enough for her, and she turned to other men. One day he found her with a slave.

He cut off both their heads with his own sword.

From that day the Sultan changed. Once he had loved one woman. Now he hated all women. "I cannot be sure of any of them," he said to his vizir. "From this time I shall marry a new wife every day, and at sunrise the next morning she must die. One day will not be long enough, even for a woman, to do wrong."

A time of great unhappiness then began for the Sultan's people. Every family lived in fear. If the Sultan asked a father for his daughter as a wife, how could the father say no? They began to hide their daughters, or send them into the country. It soon became difficult for the vizir to find new wives; and this made him afraid.

"What will the Sultan do to me when I cannot find any at all?" he thought.

Now, the vizir himself had two daughters. He was a good, loving father, and they did not like to see him look unhappy. One day, the elder, Sheherezade, said: "Father, I want you to do something for me. By doing this you will please the Sultan, the people and me."

"In the name of God," said the vizir, "I would do anything to please so many people. Ask, and I shall do it for you."

"Give me to the Sultan as a wife."

The vizir's face turned white. "Give you up to be killed? Never! You do not know what you are saying."

"Father," said Sheherezade. "Are you a true servant of God, or do you use words without thinking? You cannot say no. You said 'In the name of God', so you *must* do this for me. I want to be the Sultan's wife."

The vizir beat his head with his hands. He knew he had to do this thing. But why did she want to throw her life away?

Sheherezade went to her sister, Dunyazade, and told her what she had done. At first her sister wept, but Sheherezade kissed her and said:"Do not think I want to die. By this marriage I hope to save many girls' lives, and my own, too. But you must help me. I want you to sleep in the same room as the Sultan and myself. Wake me up one hour before sunrise and ask me to tell you a story. That is the only thing I ask."

The next day Sheherezade went with her father to the Sultan. The Sultan was pleased and surprised. He never thought his vizir would give his own daughter as a wife. But there she was. Everything was made ready, and they were married.

That night, when it was time to go to bed, Sheherezade said: "My lord, my sister has always slept in the same room as me. May she stay with me tonight – my last night?"

"She can do as you wish," said the Sultan. He was still pleased that the vizir had given him his own daughter.

Nobody slept that night. The Sultan always slept badly. Sheherezade was excited. Dunyazade was afraid. She knew she had to stay awake to save her sister's life. One hour before sunrise she spoke: "Dear sister," she said, "if you are still awake, please tell me a story."

So Sheherezade began.

CHAPTER TWO

The man who never laughed again

There was once a rich man who died, leaving everything
to his son, Salem. But Salem was too young to have so
much money. He threw it away on fine clothes, eating
and drinking, singers and dancers. When there was no
more money he sold his land and houses. In the end
there was nothing. He then had to find work carrying
things for people in the streets of the city.

One day, as he was sitting in the street waiting for
somebody to give him work, an old man came up to
him. "You have had a better place in life," he said. "I see
it in your face. I live with ten other old men in one
house. Come and be our servant. Who knows? God may
give you back part of what you lost."

The old man's house was in a part of the city Salem
did not know well. Before going in, the old man turned
to him and said: "There is one thing to tell you about
this house. It is an unhappy place; but never ask the
cause."

"I shall remember that," said Salem, and he followed
the old man through the door.

Although the house looked poor outside, inside it was
very beautiful. The rooms had high ceilings and floors
of coloured stone. In the middle was a lovely garden. At
first Salem could only hear the sound of running water
and the song of birds. But as he stood there, other
sounds came to his ears – sounds of weeping from the
other old men. All dressed in black, they were praying in

their rooms.

The first old man took him into his own room. There he showed him a box filled with gold. "Take from this box what you need for our needs and for yours," he said.

Salem also noticed a door in that room, locked with many locks. But he did not ask what was behind it. This was not a house where one asked questions.

Years passed, and Salem served his masters well. One by one, the old men died, and were buried in the garden by the others. At last only one remained – the one who had first taken Salem in. When he, too, fell ill, Salem said: "If you now die, I shall never know the cause of your great unhappiness."

"My son," said the old man, "let that die with me. But I will tell you one thing before it is too late. If you want to remain happy, do not try to open the locked door."

Soon after that, he died, and Salem became the owner of the house and the money. But although he was quite rich again, he was not happy. He could not stop thinking about the old men. He also thought about the locked door. What could be behind it? Surely opening a door could not hurt anyone?

At last, Salem could not bear these thoughts even for one more day. He took a piece of heavy iron and broke off all the locks. The door fell open.

Sheherezade stopped.

"Well?" said the Sultan. "What *was* behind the door?"

"My lord," said Sheherezade, "there is already light in the sky, and I must die."

"But you cannot stop there. The story is unfinished."

"My lord, if you will give me another day ..."

The Sultan looked angry. Outside in the palace yard a slave with a long sword waited. At last the Sultan said: "I will give you one more day. But after that ..."

The next night, Sheherezade went on.

———————

Perhaps Salem had hoped to find more gold. But there was nothing like that behind the door – only a dark, narrow passage. So he took a lamp, and followed it deep down into the earth. It seemed like hours before he saw daylight again. But at last the passage opened out into a cave. In a few minutes he was standing beside the sea.

As he stood there, not knowing what to do, he saw something in the sky. It got bigger and bigger. It was a giant bird flying straight towards him. Catching him by his clothes, it carried him up and flew off over the sea.

The bird flew on all through the night, and Salem forgot his fear and slept. Early next morning they came to an island. The bird flew lower, and Salem could see a lot of people. They stood there as if they were waiting for him.

Down flew the bird, right into the middle of them, and left him there. Suddenly people were all round him. Some came up and put a crown on his head; others helped him get on to a fine horse. Then, with soldiers in front, and soldiers behind, Salem was taken through lovely gardens to a palace. They led him inside to a

room with two jewelled chairs; and in one of them sat the most beautiful woman he had ever seen.

As Salem came in, she rose, and said: "I am the queen of this island. I have waited so long, but you have come at last, and I am happy now."

She took him by the hand and led him off to the palace and gardens. "All this could be yours," she said. Salem knew that she wanted him to be her king.

"I would like this," he said.

"Only one thing is not for you," she went on, as they came back to the first room. She pointed to a door in the corner, which he had not noticed before. "Do not open it, or you will be unhappy all the days of your life."

"Why should I wish to?" said Salem, taking her hand. "Everything I ever wanted is here in this room."

Salem married the queen, and they lived happily for many years. At first he never thought about the door at all. But as time passed, he began to notice it more and more.

"The old man told me not to open the first door," he said to himself. "But I did, and it led me to this island and my queen. What might this door lead me to?"

One day his wish to know became too strong. He jumped up from his jewelled chair. The door was not even locked. He threw it open.

At first everything was dark. But as he went on looking, he seemed to see a large, shining eye; then a head; then a feathery body. It was the bird that had brought him to the island!

Suddenly it jumped out into the room. Salem tried to hide behind his chair. But the bird caught hold of him, and pulled him outside into the palace yard. As it flew up into the air, the palace became smaller and smaller. Then the bird started out over the sea, and the whole island passed away into cloud.

A day and a night went by. Then Salem woke up suddenly as his feet touched the ground. The bird flew up again, leaving him on the sand by the sea. It was just the place where the bird had carried him off many years before.

For months Salem walked up and down by the sea, asking sailors to take him back to the island. But nobody knew anything about it. In the end he understood. No ship could ever take him back. He had lost his queen for ever. Now at last he knew the cause of the old men's sadness. They, too, had made the same journey.

He went back to the city. The house of the old men still stood. There he lived for the rest of his life. He prayed; he wept; and he never laughed again.

CHAPTER THREE

The Caliph laughs

"That was a sad story," said the Sultan, when Sheherezade had finished. "But there is little in this sad world to laugh about." Like Salem he did not laugh any more.

"But is the world so sad?" asked Sheherezade. "Even great men must laugh sometimes. I could tell you a story of one who did – the great Caliph Haroun. Like you, my lord, he could not sleep; and one night, sitting with his vizir, he suddenly cried out – oh, but I cannot tell you what he cried out. It is too late."

"But I want to know," said the Sultan. "I think I can give you one more day. You will tell me the story tonight."

So that night Sheherezade went on.

Suddenly the Caliph cried out: "The night is long. What can I do to make it shorter?" Just then Masrour, the big black slave who watched over him night and day, began to laugh.

The Caliph was angry. "What!" he cried. "Do you laugh because your master cannot sleep? Or is your mind going soft as you get old?"

"My lord," said Masrour, "of course I was not laughing at you. I was just thinking, and I could not stop myself. You see, yesterday I walked down to the River Tigris. There I saw a lot of people standing round a big fat man. He was talking to them and making them laugh. I was thinking of some of the things he said. That is why I laughed."

Now, when Haroun could not sleep, he would do anything to make the hours pass. So he said to Masrour: "Go and find this man. He made you laugh; he may make me laugh, too."

So Masrour went off into the night and found the house where the fat man lived. At first the man, whose name was Abdurrazak, did not want to get up. But when he heard it was the Caliph who wanted him, he dressed quickly and came outside. "Let us go, then," he said. "We must not keep a great man waiting."

Masrour held him back. "Wait," he said. "If you make the Caliph laugh, he will give you money. But think. Who told him about you? It was me, Masrour. So whatever he gives you, you keep a quarter, and I take three-quarters."

"Oh, no," said Abdurrazak. "I keep three-quarters and you get a quarter."

This went on for some time. But in the end it was made clear that Abdurrazak would have one-third, and Masrour two-thirds. Then they went on to the palace.

"I have heard," said Haroun, "that you can make people in the street laugh. But now let us see. Can you make a Caliph laugh?"

So Abdurrazak began to say and do funny things. Masrour soon began to laugh. Next the vizir laughed. This man could surely make a donkey laugh.

But not the Caliph. His face showed no feelings. Abdurrazak was at first surprised. Then, when the Caliph

still did not laugh, he began to feel afraid.

At last, Haroun spoke: "I have had enough of this foolishness. You will now be paid for it. Masrour, beat this man nine times with a stick."

So Masrour took a stick and started to beat the unhappy Abdurrazak. One ... two ... three ... Then Abdurrazak cried out: "I have had my third. The rest is yours, Masrour. Give me the stick.''

Masrour stopped.

"What is the matter?" asked the Caliph. "What is this 'third'?" Then Masrour had to tell him what they had planned to do.

"Do you wish to keep your two-thirds?" asked the Caliph.

"No, no, my lord. I do not want it. This man can take it all."

"Go on, then," said the Caliph. "And, Vizir, remember: Masrour's two-thirds must go to Abdurrazak."

By the time Masrour's stick had fallen for the ninth time, Abdurrazak only wanted to get away from the palace as quickly as he could. But the Caliph called to him and said: "Do not go yet. That was only the first part of your payment."

When he heard this, Abdurrazak's face turned green. What other punishment did the Caliph have for him?

"This is the second part," the Caliph went on. "My vizir will give you ninety gold dinars." He turned to look at Masrour's unhappy face. Now at last, and for the first time that night – the Caliph laughed.

"I liked that," said the Sultan, when Sheherezade had finished. "But it was short, and there is time for another story. Your last story made a Caliph laugh. This time, let us see what you can do for a Sultan."

So Sheherezade began her next story.

CHAPTER FOUR

The story of the helpful barber

There was once a rich young man of Baghdad called Faisal. Although he had a big house with many servants, he did not have a wife. He did not feel happy in the company of women; and love, he thought, was just foolishness.

One day, while in the town, he saw coming towards him a lot of laughing women. He did not want to meet them, so he turned into a side street, and as he stood there waiting for them to pass, he noticed someone at a window across the street. A girl was just going to water some flowers. But when his eyes met hers, she moved away inside.

In less than a minute, Faisal's whole life changed. He had just seen the most beautiful girl in the world – or so he thought. He stood there, hoping she might come back, but she did not. Then a man on a horse, followed by several servants, came into the street. He stopped outside the girl's house and went inside. "Is this her father?" Faisal said to himself.

Faisal went home. He laid himself down on his bed, not sleeping and not eating. His servants could do nothing to make him happier. At last an old woman, who sometimes came to the house asking for food, came up. She looked at him and said: "It is love that makes him behave like that. Tell me, my son, who is it that has stolen your heart away?"

Then Faisal turned over and told her everything.

"Oh, my son," she said. "She is the daughter of the chief judge. He will not easily let her marry even a rich young man like you. But do not lose hope. They know me in that house. Let me go to the girl and see what can be done."

So the old woman went round to the judge's house – weeping as she went.

"Why, what is the matter, old mother?" asked the girl, when she saw the old woman's red eyes. "Why are you so unhappy?"

"Ah," she said. "I am not weeping for myself. I am weeping for a poor young man who is going to die."

"Who is he?" asked the girl. "And why must he die?"

The old woman then told her about Faisal. Of course, she said he was richer than he really was, and better– looking, and of better family. But that, as you know, is how all these old women try to make marriages.

Now, the daughter was tired of being locked up by her father. She was quite old enough to be married, and wanted to see this young man. So she said: "On Friday my father goes to the morning prayers. Let the young man come then, and I will speak with him."

When Friday came, Faisal was very excited. First he went to the bath. Then he sent his boy into the town to find a barber. The boy was slow, but in the end he found one, and brought him back to the house.

By now, time was passing, and Faisal wanted to be ready. But this barber seemed to think he had all day. He laid out his things; told a not very funny story; cut a few hairs; talked about his brother's wife's father's illness; cut a few more hairs; said what a good barber he was; and so the man went on. Faisal became tired of this fool's talk. "Be quick," he said. "I have to visit friends."

"Friends!" cried the barber suddenly. "Now I remember. I asked some friends to eat with me today, and I have not bought any food. What will they think of me?"

"Look," said Faisal, "I am going out. I do not need the food I have in the house. Take it all, but finish your work and GO!"

"Master," said the barber. "How can I ever thank you enough? What can I do for you? I know! I will walk with you as far as your friend's door."

Then Faisal got really angry. "You go to your friends, and I will go to mine. I need no company where I am going."

"Ah!" said the barber, waving a finger at him. "I think you are going to see a lady friend. That is why you want to go alone. Am I not right? But if that is so, I am just the man to take with you. I have helped so many of my friends in this way. I know what difficulties you may meet."

The barber by then was getting excited, and Faisal was afraid that his servants would hear him. So he said: "Go, take the food home to your friends. I will wait for you, and we will go together to my friends." In this way he hoped to get away from the man.

It was late when he got to the girl's house, and prayers had already started in the mosque. The old woman let him in and led him up the stairs to a fine room. He sat down on the floor and waited for her to bring the girl in.

Almost at once he heard an angry voice below. It was the chief judge! Coming home early, he had found a servant doing something wrong. He started to beat the man, who cried out in pain.

Now, the barber had not gone home. He never believed that Faisal was going to wait for him. So he had paid a man to take the food home, while he followed Faisal to the judge's house. As he waited outside in the street, he heard the servant's cries, and thought that the judge had found Faisal. He began to beat on the door. "Help! Help!" he cried. "They are killing my master."

Hearing this noise, some people came out of their houses. Others, coming back from the mosque, also stopped. Soon more than a hundred people stood round the judge's door, and they all began to cry: "Help! Help! They are killing his master."

The judge heard the noise and opened the door. He was surprised and a little frightened to see so many people. Then the barber pushed himself forward and said: "What have you done with my master?"

"What have you done with his master?" shouted the people. They were getting excited.

"But who is his master?" asked the judge. "And why is he in my house?"

"You bad old man," said the barber. "You know my master loves your daughter. You have killed him for trying to see her."

"Good people," said the judge, "my house is open to all. But I tell you, this man's master is not inside."

So the barber led the people into the judge's yard. Faisal heard them coming, and looked for a place to hide. But just as he was climbing into a box, the barber came in. "Master," he said, "I shall save you yet." And while everybody was running all over the house, he started to carry the box down to the yard.

"You fool," said Faisal from inside. "I need someone to save me from *you*." He was so angry that he kicked the side of the box; the barber missed a step, the box fell down the stairs, and Faisal climbed out with a broken arm. Although he felt great pain, he pushed his way through the people in the yard into the street.

Even when he set off home, the barber still followed him, saying: "Thanks be to God that I have saved my master. How happy I am that I was there to help him!"

———

Shahriar laughed. He had not laughed for years, but now he laughed. In the next room his vizir, waiting for his master to begin the day's work, heard him laugh; and many questions passed through his mind. "What can have made him laugh? Why is he so late in getting up? And why is Sheherezade still alive?"

That night she began a new story.

CHAPTER FIVE

The boy judge

In the time of the Caliph Haroun, a man called Ali Cogia lived in Baghdad. Ali was not rich: he was a seller of sweets and cakes. But he had no wife and family to look after, and had enough for his own needs.

Under the floor of the room at the back of his shop he kept a jar; and every week he put a small gold piece into it. The money was for him to use when he was old or ill. For, as he often said, "I have no sons to look after me when I am old and cannot work."

One day, when Ali was about fifty years old, he took out the jar and counted the money. There were more than a thousand gold pieces inside. "More than enough for the time when I am old," he said to himself, and he began to think.

Now, Ali was a good man. He went to the mosque every Friday; he gave money to the poor. But there was one thing which he had not done. He had not made the journey to Mecca.

From that day Ali thought more and more about the journey. He had the money. Poorer men than him had gone. Yet, life in Baghdad was easy, and the road to Mecca was hard. Not everyone who went there came back. But the thought had come into his head and would not go out. The time for the journey was near, and at last he said to his friends: "This year I will go."

So he sold his shop and got ready for the journey. But one difficulty remained — the jar with the gold. "Who will look after it while I am away?" he thought.

At last he thought of something. He went into a shop and bought some olives. Then he filled the jar with them so that they covered the gold. Lastly he closed the top of the jar and took it to his friend Hussein, who kept the shop next to his.

"Brother Hussein," he said, "you know that I am going, if God wishes, to Mecca. I have sold everything, and have only this jar of olives. I do not like to waste good food. Can I leave it with you till I come back?"

"That is a small thing to ask a friend," said Hussein. "Put it here in this corner of my shop. Nobody will touch it there. And may God bring you safely back to Baghdad."

After many weeks Ali reached Mecca. There he did all the things that people have to do there. Then the time came for him to leave. This was the first journey that Ali had ever made. Before, he had been afraid to travel. Now, he found that he rather liked it. So he did not go straight back home.

In Mecca he had met some Egyptian merchants. "Come back with us to Cairo," they said. "There is always work there for a maker of sweets."

So Ali went with them and stayed two years. After that he moved on to Damascus. Time passed. It was nearly seven years since he had left Baghdad.

"It is long enough," he said one day. "I shall sell my shop here and go back to my own city of Baghdad to die among my friends."

On the very day that Ali Cogia left Damascus, Hussein's wife needed some olives. There were none in the house, and the shop in their street was shut. "What shall I do?" she asked.

"There are some olives in my shop," said Hussein. "Do you remember? Seven years ago old Ali Cogia left a jar of them with me. He never came back from Mecca. Some people say he went to Cairo, but he is surely dead by now."

"So let us eat his olives," said his wife. "They are doing no good to a dead man."

Hussein went into his shop, and there, still in its corner, stood the jar. Nobody had touched it in all those seven years. But when he opened it and looked inside, he saw that the olives at the top were quite dry. He put his hand deeper into the jar, but even those lower down were dry. So he put his whole arm in. When he pulled it out, black, oily and salty, he was holding a gold piece.

He put his hand into the jar again and found more gold. Many thoughts flew round his head. At last he put the gold into the jar again and went back to his wife. To her he only said: "Those olives were too old and dry."

The next day he took the olives out of the jar and threw them away. Then he took the gold out and buried it in his yard. Next, he went and bought new olives. He filled the jar with these, and closed it as it had been before.

"Seven years is a long time," he said to himself, "but I cannot be sure that Ali Cogia is dead. If he does come back, I shall have a jar of olives to give him. And that is what he asked me to look after – a jar of olives."

A few weeks later Ali Cogia came back to Baghdad. The first thing he did was to go round to Hussein's house. After they had talked for some time, Ali asked him about the jar of olives.

"Olives?" said Hussein. "What olives?"

"You remember. Before I left, I gave you a jar of olives to keep for me," said Ali. "You put it in a corner of your shop."

"Ah, perhaps you did give me a jar," said Hussein. "I had forgotten. Seven years is a long time. Let us go into my shop and see if it is still there."

Hussein's words had made Ali feel afraid. But when he saw the jar, just where he had left it, he felt much better. "My friend," he said, "you have looked after this jar for seven years. Now I want to give you something. You will see what is in the jar which you have kept so well."

With these words Ali put his arm into the jar and pulled out – not the gold pieces which he wanted to give to Hussein – but olives. He tried again and again, but the same thing happened every time.

"Where is my gold?" he asked at last.

"Gold? What gold?"

"The gold I put in this jar."

"You said nothing about a jar of gold. You only gave me this jar of olives."

"My friend, if you needed the money, do not be afraid to say. You may pay it back, a little every week, but ..."

"I have not touched your jar, and know nothing of any gold ..."

At last, after this had gone on for some time, Ali said: "Enough. I shall go to the judge. He will know which of us is telling the truth, and the law will punish the other."

"I don't mind," said Hussein. "Let us see if the judge is foolish enough to believe the story you have just told me."

The next day Ali and Hussein took the matter to the judge.

"Did anyone see you put the gold in the jar?" the judge asked Ali.

"No, I was alone. I have no wife or family."

"Did you tell anybody about putting the gold in the jar?"

"No, I did not want anybody to know."

"What did you tell Hussein was in the jar?"

"Olives."

Then the judge turned to Hussein. "Did anyone tell you there was gold in this jar?"

"No."

"Did you at any time open the jar?"

"No."

"Ali Cogia," said the judge, "how can you waste our time in this way? There is nothing to show that there was ever any gold in your jar. You are an old man. You do not remember what you did seven years ago."

Ali was angry at the judge's words. But there was one more thing he could do. He wrote a letter to the Caliph about the whole matter, and gave it to one of the Caliph's servants.

By this time the story of the jar of olives had passed through all the markets of Baghdad. Everybody was talking about it, some believing Ali, and others believing Hussein. So when the Caliph got Ali's letter, he read it with care. He liked to know everything that went on in the city.

That night he called for his vizir and said: "Let us put on plain clothes tonight and walk about the streets. I want to hear what people are saying about this Ali Cogia. Is he a fool, or a man of truth, or a thief?"

As they were walking through that part of the city where Ali lived, they heard children speak the names of Ali and Hussein.

"You can be Ali."

"Let me be Hussein."

"All right, and I shall be the judge."

The two men stopped and looked into the yard where the voices were coming from. The children were sitting under a tree playing a game. One boy was playing the judge, and two more were playing Ali and Hussein. There were others, too. As the game went on, the Caliph listened more and more carefully. The boy judge was asking good questions.

At last, the Caliph said to the vizir: "Go in and speak to this boy. Tell him to come to the palace tomorrow morning. I also want to see the judge, Ali Cogia, Hussein, two olive merchants and the jar of olives."

The next day all these people came before the Caliph. Every one of them felt afraid: the judge was afraid because he thought he might have made a mistake; Ali was afraid because the Caliph might think he was a thief; Hussein was afraid because he *was* a thief; the merchants were afraid because they did not know what the Caliph might know about them, and the boy was afraid because he had never seen such a wonderful palace before.

"Come, boy," said the Caliph. "Sit down beside me. I heard you judge these two men in play last night. Today you shall really do it. – And you," he said to the judge, "listen to this child and learn how to tell truth from un-truth, right from wrong, and good men from thieves."

Although still afraid, the boy spoke clearly. "Bring me the jar," he said. And the jar was put before him. "Is this the jar you gave to your friend?"

"Yes," said Ali.

"Is this the jar that Ali gave to you?"

"Yes," said Hussein.

The boy put his hand in the jar and took out some olives. He gave some to the Caliph and to Ali and Hussein. Then he slowly ate one himself. "They are very good olives," he said.

Then to Hussein he said: "Did you eat any of them before today?"

"Not one," he answered. "I did not touch that jar from the time it came into my shop to the day Ali Cogia came back to Baghdad."

The boy then turned to the olive merchants. "You try them," he said. "They are good olives, although seven years old."

"Seven years old?" cried one of the merchants. "I can see by looking at them that they are not so old. They are this year's olives. No olive is any good after three years."

"Even after two years they lose their colour," said the second merchant.

"And yet Hussein says that these olives have been in the jar for seven years," said the boy.

"I have bought and sold olives for twenty years," said the first merchant, "and I know that olives do not last for seven years."

Hussein's face had gone white. His eyes were turned to the ground. "I took the gold," he said. "It is in a hole in my yard."

The Caliph then spoke: "You know how the law punishes thieves."

But before Hussein could answer, Ali said: "O great Caliph, do not cut off his hand. He was once a good friend to me. I did wrong to leave the gold with him. Let him go with a beating."

The Caliph looked at the boy judge. "A beating would be enough," the boy said.

"Then let it be so," said the Caliph.

So Hussein kept his hand, but lost his good name; Ali lost a friend, but got back his gold; and the boy judge was sent by the Caliph to study law. For as the great Haroun said: "Twenty jars of gold cannot buy a good judge."

CHAPTER SIX

The dwarf and the fishbone

"It is hard to find out the truth," said the Sultan at the end of the story. "Who would want to be a judge?"

"It was even harder to find the truth about the dwarf of Basra," Sheherezade answered. "But you surely know that story. And even if you did not, there is no time to tell it ..."

"There is time to tell the story, and time to cut off your head. You have one more day."

The next night, Sheherezade went on.

There once lived, in the city of Basra, a fish merchant. He was a rough but friendly man who liked good company. After shutting up his shop at night, he used to walk round the city looking for people to talk to. If he found someone who could make him laugh, he often asked him home to eat.

One day, on one of these walks, he met a dwarf, who told him some very funny stories. "Come home," he said to the dwarf, "and tell me more. My wife is cooking a big fish. You can help us eat it."

So they went in and sat down to dinner. The fish smelt good; the dwarf was hungry; and the merchant's wife gave him more and more. "You are little only because you do not eat enough," she said. "We will turn you into a giant before you leave this house."

The merchant laughed when he heard his wife say

this, and struck the dwarf on the back. He only did this in a friendly way, but it ended badly. The food in the dwarf's mouth went down too quickly – and a fishbone went down with it. The bone stuck at the back of his mouth. He could not speak. He got up. His face turned red, then blue. At last he fell backwards on to the floor.

The merchant was afraid. "I do not want a dead man in my house," he said. "There will be questions. They will take me to the judge. He will say I was the cause of his death, and what will happen then?"

"We must get him out of the house," said his wife.

The merchant thought for a little. Then he carried the dwarf's body outside. Across the road on the first floor lived a doctor. He climbed the doctor's stairs and sat the dwarf down on the top step. Then he beat on the door and ran back to his own house.

The doctor was waiting for a friend to come. Hearing a noise outside, he ran to the door and threw it open. But as he did so, the door hit the dwarf, who fell right to the bottom of the stairs.

"What have I done?" cried the doctor, as he ran down the stairs. The dwarf was not moving; he did not seem to be breathing. "What will people say about a doctor who kills people even before he has looked at them? Nobody will ever come to me again."

He looked up and down the street. It was late, and nobody was out. In the next house lived an old man who sold birds. Why not throw the body over the wall, and let him deal with it?

The body was not heavy. It went over the wall easily and came down on a cage of birds. The cage fell over, and the birds began to make a noise.

This old birdseller had been visited by thieves several times. So when he heard his birds make a sudden noise, he took a thick stick and went outside. He soon found the cage on its side. Behind it he could just see someone's head. He raised his stick and brought it down hard.

"Take that, you thief!" he cried. "Come out and show me what you've got."

The "thief" did not move. So the old man laid his hands on him and pulled him out. "Come on," he said. "Tell me what you are doing here." But the dwarf had nothing to say.

The old man began to feel afraid. He looked at the

body more closely. There did not seem to be any life in it. "Surely I did not hit him *so* hard," he said to himself. "But he is very small. To beat a thief is one thing: to kill him is another. What will the judge say?"

He unlocked the door of his yard and looked outside. There was nobody walking about. He quickly carried the body down the street to a big house near the corner. There he laid it in front of the door, and placed the dwarf's head on his arm as if he was asleep. Then he ran home.

The owner of this house was a rich man. The other people in the street kept away from him, because he was always angry. They all knew when he was at home, because they could hear him shouting at his wife, his sons or his servants.

Now, that night he had gone out to dinner. He had eaten too much and quarrelled with his friends. So when he came back home and found someone sleeping in front of his door, he let out an angry cry. He began to kick the dwarf. "Are there no other doors in the street, but mine?" he shouted. "Wake up!"

The dwarf did not wake up, but the other people in the street did. They looked out of their windows, and saw the man kicking the dwarf. At last one of them went into the street and said: "You will kill that little man, if you go on like that."

The rich man stopped. He looked down at the dwarf, who had not moved all this time.

"Look," said the other man, bending down to look at the body. "I told you not to kick him. He's dead. You've killed him."

Then all the people looking out of their windows said: "He's killed him! He's killed him! Take him to the judge!"

So although it was still night, they all went off to the judge's house, taking the dwarf with them. The judge got up. He looked at the dwarf. He listened to what the people had to say. Then he asked the rich man to show what he had done. So the rich man walked up to the dwarf and kicked him.

"It is enough to cause death to such a little man," said the judge "For this you, too, must die."

Now, among the many people present was the bird-seller. When he heard the judge's words, he thought: "If I let this man die, surely God will punish me. I must tell the truth." So he said to the judge: "This man did not kill the dwarf. He was already dead when he kicked him. The dwarf came into my yard to steal my birds, so I hit him with this stick, and he died. Afterwards I left the body by this man's door."

Then the judge asked him to show what he had done. So the old man went up to the dwarf and hit him on the head with his stick.

"If you killed him," said the judge, "it is you who must die."

When he heard this, the doctor spoke up: "Don't go so fast. It was not the old man who killed the dwarf, but me. I opened my door too quickly and pushed the dwarf down the stairs. It happened like this."

He pulled the dwarf to his feet, and pushed him over on to the floor again. "Afterwards I put the body in the old man's yard. I do not like this old man with his noisy, smelly birds, but I cannot let him die for this."

"Will we ever get to the end of this?" asked the judge. "So it is you who must die."

"Not so," said the fish merchant. "It was I who killed the dwarf and no other person." Then he told his story.

"Show us how it happened," said the judge. So the fish merchant sat the dwarf up and then hit him in the back. But as he did this, the bone jumped out of the dwarf's mouth. He began to breathe again and opened his eyes. He was not dead at all!

"Ow! Ow!" he cried, as he felt all the parts of his body that had been pushed, pulled, kicked and beaten. "Where am I?"

Then the judge spoke for the last time. "Because the dwarf is still alive, I cannot put anyone to death. But for what you have done to him you must each pay him fifty gold dinars. I shall say nothing about what you tried to do to each other. But I know this. I would not live in your street, among such people, for five thousand dinars."

Sheherezade's next story was a long one, and went on for two nights. The Sultan knew he was being weak in letting her live. But he could not bear to leave a story unfinished. He just had to know what would happen next.

CHAPTER SEVEN

Ali Baba and the cave

Kasim and Ali Baba were brothers who lived in a town in Persia. Kasim, the elder, was rich, with a shop, a stone-built house and a garden. Ali Baba was only a poor woodcutter, with two donkeys, a wooden hut and a yard filled with firewood. Kasim did not see his brother very much, and passed all his time with his rich friends.

One day, when Ali Baba was in the forest cutting wood, he heard the sound of many horses. This was a place far from the town, and no traveller ever passed that way. So to Ali Baba the sound only meant one thing – thieves! He quickly drove his donkeys into the forest and climbed a tree.

It *was* thieves – forty of them; and they stopped and got down from their horses near his tree. Ali Baba was afraid. "Why have they stopped just there? Have they seen me?" he thought. He felt even more afraid when their chief walked straight towards him.

But he did not stop at the tree. He went on to a rocky side of the mountain. Then, very quietly – perhaps so that the others could not hear – he said: "Open, Sesame." The rock opened like a curtain into a big cave.

The other thieves then carried bags into the cave, and the rock closed behind them. Some time later they all came out again – this time with empty bags. The rock closed, and they all rode off.

When the forest was quiet again, Ali Baba climbed down from his tree. He walked to where the chief had

stood, and said: "Open, Sesame." Again the rock opened, and he went in.

At first he could see nothing. But after some time he began to see gold, jewels and lengths of the finest, richest cloth. Even forty thieves could not gather so much together in forty years. Surely their fathers and grandfathers had used the cave before them.

But Ali Baba did not stop to think about this. He opened the cave again with the magic words and went to find his donkeys. He filled their baskets with gold and covered it with firewood, Then at last he set off for the town.

It was late when he got home. Even there, he did not feel safe until he had carried the baskets into his hut. There he poured the gold out on to the floor, and told his story to his wife. Then he left her to count the money while he went to look at his donkeys.

His wife sat down and began to count, but she was so excited that she made mistakes all the time. "What I need," she said to herself, "is a measure. I will go to Kasim's wife for one."

Kasim's wife had a measure: she had everything. She also liked to know everything. "What do they need to measure?" she asked her servant. "They are so poor. Put a little oil in the bottom of the measure. Then whatever she measures will stick to it, and we shall know what it is."

Ali Baba's wife went off with the measure, measured the gold, and took it back. She did not notice one small gold piece stuck to the bottom. But Kasim's wife did. She took it to Kasim.

"You think we are rich," she said, "but we are not as rich as your brother. He has so much money that he doesn't count it. He measures it!"

Kasim took the gold piece and went to his brother's house. He had not been there for two years. "Dear brother," he said, "you left this gold piece in our measure. I am glad that you have so much money that you cannot count it. Tell me how you became so rich. Not by cutting firewood, I think."

At first Ali Baba said nothing. But Kasim would not go without an answer; and in the end Ali Baba told him everything. When he heard about the cave, Kasim wanted to go there himself. The next morning he took twenty donkeys and went off alone into the forest.

Everything happened as Ali Baba had said. He found the rock; he said the magic words; the cave opened; he went inside, and the cave closed again. For Kasim it was like a dream. He could think of nothing but gold. He carried twenty donkey-loads of it to the mouth of the cave. Now he only had to open the cave and load his donkeys. He stood in front of the rock and opened his mouth. But no words came. Sudden fear took hold of him. In his excitement he could not remember the magic words!

"Open rock!" he said, but nothing happened. "Open mountain! Open cave!" He tried a hundred ways to make the rock open, but it did not move.

Outside the sound of horses again filled the air. The thieves had come back and found twenty donkeys there. The chief called his men together. "Twenty donkeys outside may mean twenty men inside," he said. "When the cave opens, run at them suddenly and kill them all."

The cave opened and the thieves ran in. There was only Kasim there. They cut him down with their swords before he had time to speak, or they had time to think.

"Cut his body into four pieces," said their chief, "and leave them just inside the mouth of the cave. That will frighten away any others who may know about this place."

They did this and then they rode off, taking Kasim's donkeys with them.

Night came, but Kasim did not come home. At last his wife went to Ali Baba and asked him to go out and look for him. So he got his donkeys ready and started off for the forest again, riding through the night.

It was not quite morning when he arrived at the cave. But it was light enough to see blood on the ground. It was no surprise, then, when he opened the cave and found his brother dead. But there was no time for weeping. The thieves might not be far away, so he put the body in the donkey baskets and returned home.

It was then that his difficulties began. Ali Baba did not want people to know how his brother had died. They would ask questions. Who killed him? Where? Why? Soon the whole town would know about the cave.

But Kasim's wife had a servant who always knew what to do. This girl, Marjana, went to a man in the town who sold medicines. "My master is ill," she said. "Please give him something to make him better."

The story quickly went round that Kasim was ill.

The next day she was back again. "My master is no better, and I am afraid he will die. Give me some stronger medicine," she said. Later that day Kasim's wife and

Marjana began to cry as if in pain. Then all the people living near them knew that Kasim was dead. But none of them knew how he had really died.

The next difficulty was burying the body.

"What will people say if they notice that his body is in four pieces?" thought Ali Baba.

Again Marjana thought of something. In the town there was an old shoemaker who could not see. That night she went to his house and gave him gold. "Come with me, and I will give you more," she said. "I have something for you to sew."

She led him back to the house, and there he worked all night sewing Kasim together again. The next day the body was buried, and nobody knew that anything was wrong.

Ali Baba and his wife moved into Kasim's house, and they all lived happily together as one family. But the story did not end there. If Ali Baba and his family were happy, others were not. I mean the forty thieves ...

CHAPTER EIGHT

Ali Baba and the forty thieves

When the thieves next came to the cave, they saw that the body had gone.

"Some other person knows about our cave!" said their chief. "It must be a friend of the man we killed. But the question is, who was *he*? We killed him before we could ask him. Now there is only one way to know. One of us must go to the town and ask about a man who has been buried there in four pieces."

So one of the thieves rode to the town and talked to all the people that he knew. But all those who had died in the past few weeks seemed to have died because they were ill: not because somebody had cut them up into four pieces.

One day, the thief was standing in the market, watching the old shoemaker at work. "Ah, Baba Mustafa," he said. "You sew better than men who can see."

"It is true," said the old man. "There is nothing that I cannot sew. Why, I could even sew a man together, if you asked me."

"A man?" said the thief. "I don't believe you could do that."

"I tell you, I have sewn a man together – and not long ago."

"Take this gold," said the thief, "and tell me where you did this. If I lead you through the streets, can you remember the way?"

The old man was ready to try. Led by the thief, he at

last stopped outside Kasim's house. He put his hands on the door. "This was the house," he said.

The thief marked the house with a little cross, and took the old man home. That night he was back in the forest telling the other thirty-nine his story.

One evening, a few weeks later, a man came to the door of Kasim's house. He had with him twenty donkeys, each carrying two big oil jars.

"Good sir," he said, "I have oil to sell in the market tomorrow, but the place where the merchants stay is full. Could I leave these jars in your yard tonight?"

"God has sent a traveller to our door," said Ali Baba. "Bring in your donkeys and your jars. You must eat with us and stay the night."

The merchant thanked him, and brought his donkeys in.

Now, as Marjana was cooking the dinner, her lamp began to go out. So she looked into her jar and found that, too, was empty. Then she thought of all the oil in the yard. "Surely, the merchant will not mind if I take a little oil for my lamp," she thought. So she went outside to the nearest jar. But how surprised she was when she heard a voice from the jar ask: "Is it time?"

Thinking quickly, Marjana answered in a deep voice: "Not yet, but soon." As she went from jar to jar, she heard the same question, and gave the same answer. Only the last jar really had oil in it.

The girl knew that something was wrong. "These are the forty thieves, and the merchant is their chief," she thought. She brought all the oil from the full jar into the kitchen, and put it over the fire until it was boiling.

Then she went round to every jar and poured a little of the boiling oil into each. In this way she killed thirty-nine of the forty thieves.

But the most dangerous thief was still alive. The chief was just then sitting down with her master. Marjana served them with food. Then everybody went to bed – everybody but her. She stayed awake in her kitchen to see what this man would do.

At last she heard the thief come down into the yard.

He went to the first jar and said: "It is time." But there was no answer. He looked inside, and jumped back in fear. He went to the next jar; he ran from jar to jar until he came to the last one, which was now empty.

Just then Marjana began to make a noise in the kitchen. Not wanting to be seen, the thief climbed into the empty jar. This was just what Marjana wanted. She carried the last of the boiling oil to the jar and poured it in.

The next morning she told Ali Baba what she had done.

"You have saved us all," he said, "and there is only one way to thank you. You shall marry my own son."

So she did; and this time Ali Baba and his family really did live happily ever after.

At the end of the story the Sultan said to Sheherezade: "Men are such fools. Girls like Marjana can make them do anything. They will not see where these girls are leading them. I hope you are not a girl like Marjana."

"Oh, no, my lord. I only live to do what my lord wishes."

"Then, your lord wishes to hear another story tonight."

Sheherezade noticed that he now said nothing about the cutting off of heads. For the first time she was beginning to feel safe. "Then I shall tell you one, my lord," she said.

CHAPTER NINE

The man who turned into a donkey

Two men, who lived by stealing, were once standing in a city street. As they watched the people pass, one said to the other: "Look at them. Every day they fill the streets of the city – so many people, so many fools. Why, I could steal the clothes off their own backs and they would thank me for it."

"You think you can do anything," said the other man. "You talk about doing things, but can you really do them? I do not think men are such fools. Look at that man leading a donkey along the street. Let me see you steal his donkey *and* make him thank you for it."

"With a little help from you I can do it," said the first thief.

So they followed the man with the donkey until they came to a place where the street became very narrow and everyone had to move slowly. First the thief came up beside the donkey. Next, he gently pulled the rope off the donkey's head and waved to his friend to take the animal away. Lastly he put the rope over his own head and followed the donkey's owner along the street. This man, thinking of other things, did not know that he now had a man in place of a donkey.

The thief waited long enough for his friend to get away. Then he suddenly stopped in the way that donkeys often do. The man pulled at the rope, but the thief did not move. When at last the man turned round, his mouth fell open and his eyes opened wide.

"But who are you?" he cried.

"Oh, sir, do not ask who I am, but what I was," said the thief. "I was your donkey, but now I am a man again. Just listen to my story, and when you have heard it, you will thank God, as I do now." Then he fell down on his knees in the street and began to pray.

At last he got to his feet again and said: "Once I lived with my mother, a good old woman, who loved and feared God. But I was not like her. I lived to please myself, and did not follow God's laws.

"One night I came home late. I had taken strong drink and did not know what I was doing or saying. Once again my mother asked me to live a better life. But I had heard all this before, and I became angry. I began to beat her with a stick – my own mother. But then she, too, became angry and said: 'I see you will never change. You are like a donkey that will not cross a bridge. If you want to behave like a donkey, may God turn you into one.'

"As soon as she said those words I felt a change come over me. My ears became longer, my arms turned into legs; and when I tried to cry out, I could only make donkey noises. God had given my mother her wish.

"I ran outside into the street, not knowing where to go. The next morning a man caught me and sold me in the market – to you, sir. Then a very bad time began for me. Sometimes you beat me. Sometimes you did not give me enough food. Sometimes you gave me too much to carry. But I forgave you. I knew that it was God's punishment, and God is just.

"Then today, as I was walking along the street behind you, I suddenly heard a voice. It was the voice of my old mother praying to God to forgive me. God heard the prayer, and so I became a man again, still walking behind you at the end of a rope."

When he heard all this, the owner of the donkey said: "There is no power but the power of God! Oh, my brother, how many times have I treated you badly? Forgive me. I did not know you were a man. Here, take this money, buy yourself food and drink, and go home to your poor old mother again."

So the thief went off, very pleased with his morning's work.

When the owner of the donkey got home, his wife was surprised to see him alone. "Where is your donkey?" she asked.

"Donkey?" said the man. "We have no donkey. Nor did we ever have one." Then he told her the thief's story.

She, too, was a very simple woman. "May God forgive us," she said, "for using a man as an animal for so long. You did right to give him money. But you cannot do your work without a donkey. Tomorrow you must go to the market and buy another one."

So the next morning the man went off to the donkey market and looked round for a good strong beast. He had not gone far before he noticed a certain animal which he had surely seen before. It was his own donkey standing there for sale. For a time he did not know what to think. Then he went up to it, and spoke quietly into its long brown ear: "So you have been drinking again, and beating your poor old mother. God may forgive you. But I shall never buy you again."

———————

"That was a good story," said the Sultan. "But the night is only half over. I know you have another one ready to tell me."

Of course, Sheherezade had.

CHAPTER TEN

Aladdin and the magic lamp

In one of the cities of China there once lived a poor woman and her son. This son, Aladdin, helped her with her work of making clothes. One day, as he was taking some finished clothes to someone in the next street, a man stopped him. He was well-dressed, and had quick, shining eyes. He looked at Aladdin closely.

"You must be the son of Ismael," he said.

"Ismael was my father's name," said Aladdin, "but he died long ago. Did you know him?"

"Know him?" said the man. "He was my brother. I have come all the way from Morocco to see him. But it seems I am too late."

Aladdin did not know his father had had a brother. It was a surprise to his mother, also, when he took the man home. But she gave him food, and he gave her presents. Then he said to Aladdin: "I see I am too late to help my poor brother. But I can help his son. Tomorrow you can show me the city. The day after, I will buy you a shop and make you a merchant."

The next day Aladdin took his uncle to the King's gardens just outside the city.

"Let us walk a little further," said his uncle. "The day is fine, and I would like to see the city from those hills." So they walked on, leaving the gardens and the fields far behind. Aladdin soon felt tired. But his uncle would not stop until they came to a certain rocky place. There he made a little fire, and taking some red powder from his pocket, he dropped it in.

At once there was a great noise, and a hole opened in front of them. Aladdin was afraid, and tried to run, but his uncle held his arm.

"Fool," he said. "You run away just as I am going to do you some good. Go down into that hole. You will find steps at the bottom leading to a cave. Pass through it until you come to a garden of fruit trees. Under one of these trees is a lamp which I want. Before you come back, you may take some fruit. Lastly, take this ring. It is a magic ring, and will keep you safe."

"Safe from what?" thought Aladdin, but he did not ask. By now, he was more afraid of his uncle than the hole in the ground. So down he went into the earth.

Everything looked just as his uncle had said. He found the lamp and put it into his shirt. Then he started to take some fruit. But here was a surprise. It was not fruit, but fine jewels! He quickly filled his shirt and went back to the steps.

"Give me the lamp, and I will help you up," his uncle said. But by now, the lamp was under all the jewels, and Aladdin could not easily pull it out.

"Help me up first. Then I will give it to you," he answered. But his uncle would not help him; he wanted the lamp first. Aladdin did not like this. He was afraid his uncle might take the lamp and leave him in the cave. They began to quarrel, and his uncle became very angry. There was another loud noise, and everything went black. His uncle had made the earth close over the cave again, and Aladdin could not get out.

Now, Aladdin's "uncle" was not his uncle at all, but a

magician. He had read in his books about a magic lamp that was hidden in this cave. These books also spoke of certain dangers. That was why he had used Aladdin to get the lamp. But now, at the last minute, it seemed he had lost it. So he went back angrily to Morocco.

At first Aladdin thought his uncle would come back. But after two nights in the cave he began to lose hope – until he suddenly remembered the ring. His uncle had said it was magic. But who could believe that man? The ring had not kept Aladdin safe from him – that was certain. He looked at it. Even in the dark it shone. He rubbed it to make it shine more brightly. It really *was* magic. Suddenly a djinn stood in front of him.

"I am the Djinn of the Ring," he said. "Tell me what your wishes are."

Just then Aladdin had only one wish. "I want to go home," he said.

There was the noise of a great wind, and he found himself sitting on the floor at home, telling his mother what had happened.

"But is *that* the lamp?" asked his mother, as he emptied his shirt on to the ground. "It's old and dirty. Why did that man want it so much?"

"Perhaps it is gold under all the dirt," said Aladdin. He began to rub the dirt away with his hand. But as soon as he did so, there in front of him stood another djinn, bigger than the Djinn of the Ring.

"I am the Djinn of the Lamp," he said. "Tell me what your wishes are."

Aladdin did not have to think. He had not eaten for two days. "I want my dinner," he said. The djinn went and came back at once with food on golden plates.

Every day after that, Aladdin rubbed the lamp, and the djinn brought them what they needed. But they did not move out of their small house. Nor did they go about in new clothes. Nobody knew that they ate off plates of gold.

For a time Aladdin was happy. But one day he saw the King's daughter walking in the King's gardens, and from that day he knew he could not live without her.

Now, once a week, any person could go and speak to the King. So one morning Aladdin's mother, feeling very much afraid, went to the palace with a bag. When it was time for her to speak, she knelt down and poured the jewels from the cave in front of the King.

"My lord," she said, "I bring these presents from my son. He wishes to marry your daughter."

The King and his vizir were surprised. They had never seen such fine jewels before. But who was this woman? And who was her son? The vizir was not pleased. He wanted his own son to marry the princess. So he said to the King: "These are fine jewels, it is true. But we know nothing about these people. Tell her you will give her an answer in three months."

At first Aladdin was hopeful. But after only one month had passed, he heard in the market that the princess was to be married to the son of the vizir.

The vizir was powerful, but the Djinn of the Lamp was more powerful. Aladdin thought hard; and on the night of the marriage he told the djinn just what to do.

When all the eating and drinking was over, the two young people were taken to the room where they were going to sleep. But as soon as the princess lay down, she fell into a deep sleep that lasted till morning. As for the vizir's son, when he tried to lie down, the djinn carried him off to a cupboard. There a cold wind blew on him all night.

All this happened night after night, until in the end he could take no more. If this was marriage, he did not want it. He asked for the marriage to be ended.

Aladdin's mother now returned to the King. But the vizir still did not want the princess to marry Aladdin. "First," he said, "he is not of good family. Secondly, is he really so rich? The price of a princess is more than a bag of jewels. Tell him to bring forty golden bowls full of jewels." He thought Aladdin could never find so much.

But the vizir knew nothing about the power of the djinn. The next morning Aladdin walked into the palace with forty richly-dressed servants. Each servant carried a large golden bowl filled with jewels. The King could not now say no, and Aladdin and the princess were married.

Only one more thing was needed – a palace to live in. Again Aladdin called the djinn. That night a new palace rose up beside the King's palace. There Aladdin and his princess lived in great happiness. But this happiness did not last.

Back home in Morocco, the magician was not at all happy. He could not stop thinking about the magic lamp. Was it still buried in the cave with that foolish boy? By his magic powers he could see places far away. So one day he turned his mind to the cave. But he could not see Aladdin or the lamp. He let out an angry cry: "Does this mean that the boy got out?"

The magician set out for China a second time. As

soon as he reached Aladdin's city, he put on old clothes and bought a lot of lamps. Then he went round the streets crying: "New lamps for old! ... New lamps for old!"

Everybody thought he was a fool. They came to him, laughing, with their broken old lamps, and he gave them new ones. At last, followed by a lot of people, he stopped near Aladdin's palace. Just above was the window where the princess used to sit, watching the people pass by.

"There is an old lamp in Prince Aladdin's room," she said to her servant, when she heard the magician's cry. "Take it down and see if he will really give you a new lamp for it."

As soon as the magician got his hands on the magic lamp, he dropped all the other lamps in the road. He wanted the djinn to come to him even there in the street.

"Take me, this palace and everything inside it to Morocco," he said. A cloud came down and covered the palace. When it rose again, there was nothing there.

All this time Aladdin had been out hunting. When he came back and found an empty space where his palace had been, he cried: "This is that magician's work. What shall I do?"

Just then some soldiers came up and took him to the King.

"What have you done with my daughter?" the King asked.

"I will bring her back. Only give me time to think," answered Aladdin.

"There will be quite enough time for that," said the

King. "Lock him up!"

So Aladdin was taken away and locked up. What could he do? He had lost his wife, his palace and the lamp. He did not even know where they were. But there was one thing that he had not lost. The magic ring was still on his finger. He rubbed it, and the Djinn of the Ring was there with him in his narrow little room.

"Djinn of the Ring," he cried, "bring back my palace and my princess."

But the djinn looked down at the ground and said: "I do not have that power. Only the Djinn of the Lamp can do that."

So Aladdin thought again, and said: "Then, take me to where my palace is."

This the djinn could do. Strong winds blew into the little room and carried Aladdin all the way to Morocco. Suddenly, he heard the sound of weeping. It was his princess. As soon as she saw him, tears of sadness turned to tears of happiness. She threw her arms round him. "I knew you would come at last," she said.

Then she told him how every night the magician came to the palace. He asked her to forget Aladdin and marry him. Every night he grew more angry, and the princess more afraid.

"And my lamp?" asked Aladdin. "It is a magic one. Only with its help can we save ourselves."

"He carries it with him always. I dare not try to take it from him."

"Then put something in his drink to make him sleep," said Aladdin. "I will do the rest."

Aladdin hid in the next room and waited. At last the magician came and behaved as the princess had said. But this time, she spoke sweetly to him, and gave him something to drink. Before long, he was lying on the floor deeply asleep. It was then easy for Aladdin to come in and cut off the magician's head. He took the lamp and called the djinn. "Take the whole palace back to China," he said.

So Aladdin and his princess flew back to China, where they lived happily for many years. When the King died at last, Aladdin became King in his place. And the magic lamp? Who knows where that is now? Try rubbing the next old lamp you find. It could surprise you.

"How many stories do you know?" asked the Sultan.

"Enough for a thousand and one nights."

"That will keep you alive for two years and nine months. But what will you do then?"

"I shall make up new stories."

"That means I shall never cut off your head."

"Do you want to?"

"No," said the Sultan.

Sheherezade knew then that she had saved her life and won the Sultan's love. She went on telling stories, but not out of fear. She loved the Sultan as he loved her. So she, too, found happiness in the end.

Questions

CHAPTER 1   *The Sultan and Sheherezade*

1 What did the Sultan do to his first wife?
2 Why did Sheherezade want to marry the Sultan?
3 Who was Dunyazade?

CHAPTER 2   *The man who never laughed again*

1 How did Salem become poor?
2 Where was the old man's house?
3 Where did the passage under the ground lead to?
4 How long did it take to reach the island?
5 What did the queen of the island want?
6 What did Salem find behind the second door?
7 Why had the old men been so unhappy?

CHAPTER 3   *The Caliph laughs*

1 Why did Masrour laugh?
2 How did the Caliph feel when Masrour laughed?
3 Did Masrour plan to take three-quarters or two-thirds of Abdurrazak's money?
4 How many times did Masrour beat Abdurrazak?
5 Why did the Caliph laugh in the end?

CHAPTER 4   *The story of the helpful barber*

1 "In less than a minute, Faisal's whole life changed." How did it change?
2 Whose daughter was the girl at the window?
3 How did the old woman help Faisal?
4 What did the barber do after Faisal went to the girl's house?
5 Where did Faisal hide?

CHAPTER 5   *The boy judge*

1 When did Ali Cogia live?
2 How old was he when he went to Mecca?
3 What did he do with his gold?

4 How long did he stay away from Baghdad?
5 Who did the first judge believe?
6 How long can we keep olives?

CHAPTER 6 *The dwarf and the fishbone*

1 Why did the fish merchant ask the dwarf home?
2 What happened to the dwarf during dinner?
3 Why was the merchant afraid?
4 What did the doctor think he had done to the dwarf?
5 Where did the birdseller put the dwarf?
6 Why did the rich man kick the dwarf?
7 When did the dwarf come to life again?

CHAPTER 7 *Ali Baba and the cave*

1 Which was the rich brother?
2 Where did Ali Baba hide when he heard the thieves?
3 How did the chief thief open the cave?
4 Why did Kasim's wife put oil in her measure?
5 Why couldn't Kasim get out of the cave?
6 Why did Ali Baba keep quiet about Kasim's death?

CHAPTER 8 *Ali Baba and the forty thieves*

1 Who sewed Kasim's body together again?
2 Where did the thieves hide?
3 What did they think when Marjana answered in a deep voice?
4 Who did Marjana marry?

CHAPTER 9 *The man who turned into a donkey*

1 How did the thief's friend help him?
2 What did the man's wife think about his story?

CHAPTER 10 *Aladdin and the magic lamp*

1 Where did Aladdin and his mother live?
2 What did Aladdin's "uncle" want him to do?
3 Who helped Aladdin to get out of the cave?
4 What happened when Aladdin rubbed the lamp?
5 What didn't the princess know about Aladdin's lamp?
6 Why couldn't the Djinn of the Ring bring back Aladdin's palace?

Word list

barber	*a man who cuts hair*
bury	*to put under the ground*
caliph	*a leader of all Muslim peoples*
chief	*a leader*
dinar	*Arab money*
djinn	*a magic person in Arab fairy stories*
dwarf	*a very short person*
(fish) bone	*the hard part of an animal's body*
judge	*a person who says what is right and wrong in law*
lord	*a great man*
master	*a man who has servants or slaves*
medicine	*something taken by ill people*
merchant	*a man who buys and sells*
mosque	*a building where Muslims pray*
olive	*a fruit which gives oil*
rope	
sew	*to use a needle*
slave	*someone who serves another, and is owned by him/her*
stairs	
sultan	*a Muslim leader, like a king*
vizir	*a man who helps a sultan or caliph to rule*
yard	*an open place behind a house*